Explore the Universe

THE UNIVERSE— MYSTERIES AND MARVELS

WORLD
BOOK

a Scott Fetzer company
Chicago
www.worldbookonline.com

World Book, Inc.
233 N. Michigan Avenue
Chicago, IL 60601
U.S.A.

For information about other World Book publications, visit our
Web site at **http://www.worldbookonline.com** or call
1-800-WORLDBK (967-5325).

For information about sales to schools and
libraries, call **1-800-975-3250 (United States)**,
or **1-800-837-5365 (Canada)**.

Library of Congress Cataloging-in-Publication data
The universe -- mysteries and marvels.
    p. cm. -- (Explore the universe)
    Includes index.
    Summary: "An introduction to unusual objects and
phenomena in the universe. Includes diagrams, fun facts,
glossary, resource list, and index"--Provided by publisher.
    ISBN: 978-0-7166-9546-2
    1. Cosmology--Juvenile literature. I. World Book, Inc.
QB983.U56 2010
520--dc22
                            2009042593

ISBN: 978-0-7166-9544-8 (set)
Printed in China at Leo Paper Products, LTD.,
    Heshan, Guangdong
1st printing February 2010

Cover image:
Pismis 24, the most brilliant
star in the core of nebula
NGC 6357, puzzled scientists
for years because it seemed
to be more massive than
they thought a star could be.
But a closer look by the
Hubble Space Telescope
revealed that Pismis 24, which
is about 8,000 light-years
from Earth, is really three
closely bound stars.

NASA, ESA, and J. Maíz Apellániz,
Instituto de Astrofísica de
Andalucía, Spain

CONTENTS

If a word is printed in **bold letters that look like this,** that word's meaning is given in the glossary on pages 60-61.

INTRODUCTION

The universe is an amazing place, filled with many things we understand and many others that remain quite mysterious. Human beings have always been fascinated with the sun and other stars. We have sought to understand the universe and Earth's place in it. The curiosity of early scientists led them to amazing new discoveries, despite the limitations of their instruments.

Today, advanced technologies and techniques have revealed more about the heavens than earlier scientists ever dreamed possible. New discoveries are being made every day. Yet there is still much that scientists don't know. This book explores some interesting and unusual features of our extraordinary universe.

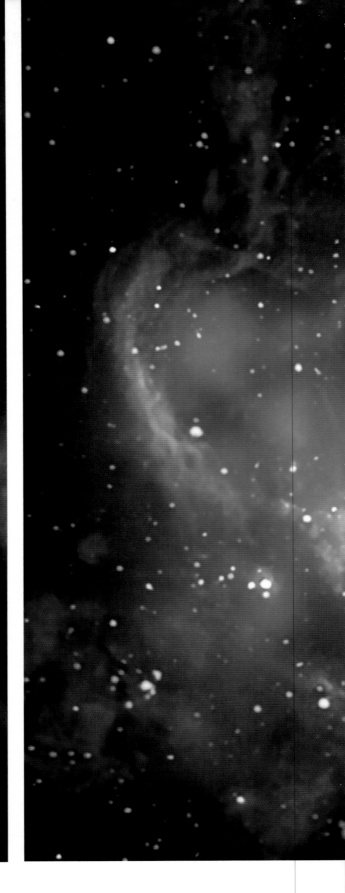

Some 200 newly created, hot, massive stars light up a large region of star formation in the galaxy M33, in a composite image from the Chandra X-ray Observatory and the Hubble Space Telescope. Vast clouds of gas and dust surrounding the stars may produce still more stars.

As vast as it seems, the solar system is an amazingly small part of an unimaginably large universe.

Solar system

Sun's neighborhood
40 light-years

The sun

INFINITE OR FINITE?

It may be impossible for anyone to measure the actual dimensions of the universe. One way scientists try to understand its size is by studying **quasars,** extremely bright objects that are considered to be some of the most distant—and oldest—objects in the universe. However, measuring the distance to a quasar does not tell us anything about the distance from one edge of the universe to another.

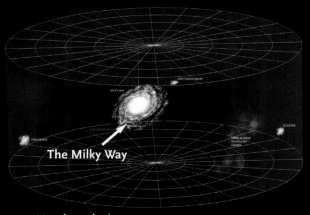

Nearby galaxies
500,000 light-years

The Milky Way

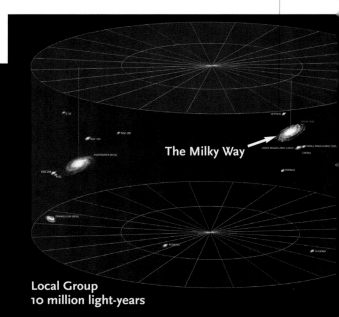

Local Group
10 million light-years

The Milky Way

The universe is so vast that even with the use of modern scientific instruments, scientists can only speculate on its size.

CONTINUING EXPANSION

Although scientists may never be able to determine the size of the universe, one thing is true: In the past, the universe was smaller than it is today. Scientists believe that the universe began about 13.7 billion years ago in an explosion called the **big bang.** Since then, the universe has expanded from a single point to its present size. It continues to expand today.

FATE OF THE UNIVERSE

Scientists have differing theories about how large the universe may become. Some think that even though the universe is immense, it will eventually reach a point where its expansion will stop. Studies of the **cosmic microwave background radiation,** the glow left over from the big bang, strongly suggest that the universe will expand forever.

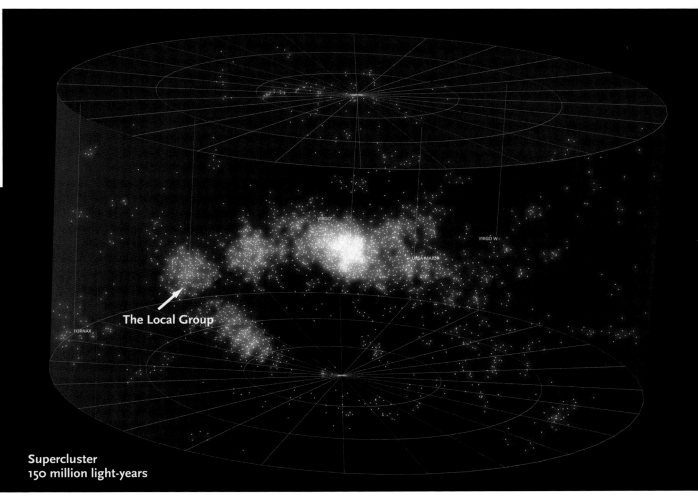

The Local Group

FORNAX

VIRGO

VIRGO W

URSA MAJOR

Supercluster
150 million light-years

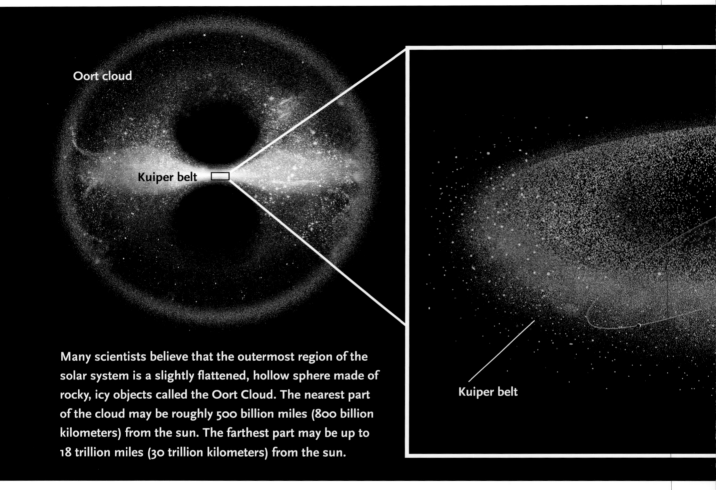

Oort cloud

Kuiper belt

Many scientists believe that the outermost region of the solar system is a slightly flattened, hollow sphere made of rocky, icy objects called the Oort Cloud. The nearest part of the cloud may be roughly 500 billion miles (800 billion kilometers) from the sun. The farthest part may be up to 18 trillion miles (30 trillion kilometers) from the sun.

Kuiper belt

OUR PLACE IN THE UNIVERSE

Strange as it may seem, we do not know where we are in the overall universe. By the 1900's, scientists had discovered that the **solar system** is part of the Milky Way **Galaxy.** However, they thought the Milky Way was the entire universe.

In the early 1900's, American astronomer Edwin Hubble discovered that the Milky Way is part of a larger collection of galaxies. This grouping of about 40 galaxies eventually became known as the Local Group.

Since then, scientists have been able to map a much larger universe stretching across billions of **light-years** and including billions of galaxies. Still, they have not been able to map the entire universe. Scientists generally agree that they probably never will be able to.

Sun

Orbit of Pluto

Orbit of Neptune

Beyond the orbit of Neptune, the farthest planet from the sun, is the Kuiper belt, another band of icy, rocky objects, including dwarf planets. Many scientists consider Pluto to be part of the Kuiper belt.

AT THE CENTER OF THE OBSERVABLE UNIVERSE

Because we cannot see the entire universe, we cannot know our exact location within it. Our situation is rather like being on a ship surrounded by ocean. Because we cannot see land, we don't know if we are in the center of the ocean or if land is just over the horizon. The solar system may lie in the middle of the universe. But because we cannot see the edge of the universe, we have no way of knowing.

Scientists, however, can see an equal distance in every direction from Earth. According to this way of thinking, each galaxy, including the Milky Way, can be considered the center of its own observable universe.

DID YOU KNOW?

The overall color of the universe has grown redder over the past 10 billion years because space continues to expand—shifting light to the redder end of the electromagnetic spectrum—and because redder (older) stars are becoming more common than bluer (younger) stars.

THE EDGE OF THE UNIVERSE

Light from the most distant **galaxies** we can observe has traveled for about 13 billion years. People sometimes say such galaxies are 13 billion **light-years** away from us, but the truth is more complicated. The galaxy may have been only about 3 billion light-years away when its light left. Because space has expanded, the light has had to cross 13 billion light-years to reach us today. The galaxy itself is now even farther away—about 30 billion light-years away. In fact, most astronomers believe that the edge of the observable universe is now about 47 billion light-years away. Beyond that edge, there are countless galaxies we will never be able to see.

Thousands of stars are visible to the unaided eye in the night sky under the right conditions. With the aid of a telescope, astronomers can view billions more.

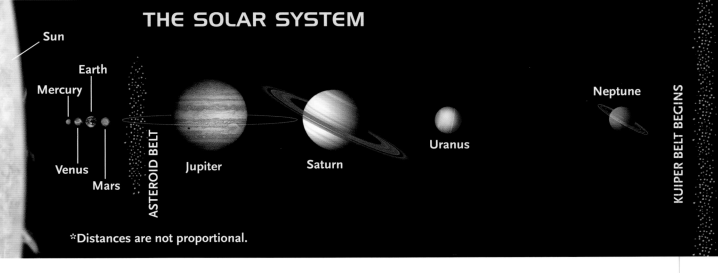

THE SOLAR SYSTEM

Sun

Earth

Mercury

Venus

Mars

ASTEROID BELT

Jupiter

Saturn

Uranus

Neptune

KUIPER BELT BEGINS

*Distances are not proportional.

The observable universe is the part of the universe that we can see with our eyes and with telescopes.

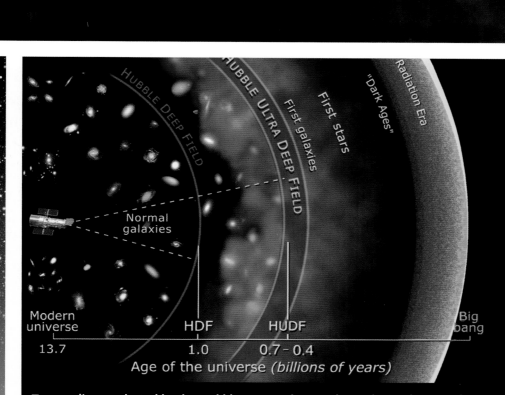

Hubble Deep Field

HUBBLE ULTRA DEEP FIELD

First galaxies

First stars

"Dark Ages"

Radiation Era

Normal galaxies

Modern universe

HDF

HUDF

Big bang

13.7   1.0   0.7 – 0.4

Age of the universe *(billions of years)*

Two studies conducted by the Hubble Space Telescope have obtained views of the universe as it appeared more than 13 billion years ago. The Hubble Deep Field showed galaxies as they appeared 12.7 billion years ago, only 1 billion years after the big bang. The Hubble Ultra Deep Field viewed galaxies that formed about 500 million years after the big bang. These galaxies are near the end of what astronomers call the observable universe, the part of the universe that we can see.

Saturn is the farthest planet we can see without a telescope. The most distant object in the solar system that can be seen with a telescope is Sedna, a dwarf planet that lies about 8 billion miles (13 billion kilometers) from the sun. Sedna may be part of the Oort cloud, a cluster of comets and smaller objects in the outermost region of the solar system.

OORT CLOUD BEGINS

DID YOU KNOW?

Light from the farthest parts of the universe will never reach us because the edges of the universe are moving away from us faster than the speed of light. More-powerful telescopes may enable us to see more of the universe, but we will never be able to see all of it.

All the objects that we can see in the night sky with the unaided eye—except one—belong to the Milky Way Galaxy. The neighboring Andromeda Galaxy can be seen on a clear night as a tiny, dim smudge of light.

OUR MILKY SKY

Nearly everything we can see in the night sky resides in the Milky Way, which is about 100,000 **light-years** in diameter. One light-year equals the distance light travels in an Earth year, which is about 5.88 trillion miles (9.46 trillion kilometers). Earth is about 26,000 light-years from the center of the **galaxy.** The portion of the Milky Way we can see appears as a broad, pearly band of starlight stretching from horizon to horizon.

Most of what we can see in the night sky without a telescope lies within a few thousand light-years from Earth.

The night sky can shine with a brilliant display of thousands of stars. However, the same night sky viewed from a city would seem dull in comparison. City lights can drown out all but the brightest stars in the night sky. The artificial light from a city is sometimes referred to as "light pollution."

On a very clear night away from the lights of a city, we can also see Andromeda, the closest large galaxy. But even on the clearest night, Andromeda looks fuzzy, like an out-of-focus **star**. Andromeda is approximately 2 million light-years away.

STAR BRIGHT

Gazing at the night sky, you've probably noticed that some stars appear brighter than others. You might conclude that the brighter the star, the closer it is to Earth. But a star that appears very bright may actually be a tremendous distance from Earth. Likewise, a faint star might turn out to be a relatively close neighbor. This is because the brightness of a star depends not only on its distance from Earth but also on the amount of light it gives off. Astronomers refer to the amount of a star's light seen on Earth, regardless of its distance, as its apparent **luminosity**.

There are billions of **galaxies** in the universe. Each galaxy may have billions of **stars**. We see stars because they give off their own **visible light**. But these objects are far from us. Their light spreads out as it moves through space, so only some of it reaches Earth.

REVEALING STARS

We see other objects, such as the moon and some **planets** in the **solar system,** because they reflect the light from the sun. As we look farther out into space, we can see clouds of dust and gas, called **nebulae,** that reflect light from nearby stars. Reflected light is much dimmer than direct light. In addition, many regions of space have almost no matter at all. These regions appear dark to us.

BYPASSING LIGHT

Finally, we see relatively little of the light that does reach Earth. Visible light created or reflected by objects in space bathes Earth. But much of this light goes unnoticed because it does not strike our eyes or the telescopes and other instruments we use to see light.

The Crab Nebula shines with light from surrounding stars and from a rotating neutron star at its core. Beams of radiation from the neutron star excite *electrons* (negatively charged particles) spinning at nearly the speed of light, creating a bluish glow.

Few types of objects in the universe actually create light. Much of the light that reaches Earth is reflected off other objects, and many regions of space have little matter to reflect light.

Light from a light bulb or a star dims quickly with distance. In general, if your distance from a light source doubles, the intensity of the light that reaches you is one-fourth as intense.

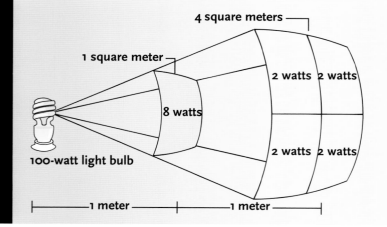

Hundreds of newly formed stars light up the Trifid Nebula, a gigantic star nursery about 5,400 light-years from Earth.

LIGHT SPEED

Light is made up of incredibly tiny particles called **photons.** They travel through space in the form of waves. Waves of light come in different **wavelengths.** A wavelength is the distance from the *crest* (top) of one wave to the crest of the next. **Ultraviolet light** has shorter wavelengths than **visible light. Infrared light** has longer wavelengths than visible light. Like matter, all forms of light are affected by **gravity.** All light moves through space at the same speed—186,282 miles (299,792 kilometers) per second.

DOPPLER REDSHIFT

Much of the light that travels through space shows **redshift.** Redshift is the change in the **spectrum** (range of wavelengths) of light from an object as the distance between Earth and that object increases. The light is stretched toward the longer, redder wavelengths of the spectrum. When an object is moving toward us, the light is pressed toward the shorter, blue wavelengths. This type of shift is called the **Doppler effect.** It is based on the movement of objects through space.

Light travels in a wave that has two parts—an electric field and a magnetic field. The two fields travel in the same direction but at right angles to each other. The amplitude of the waves is a measure of the power of the waves. The greater the amplitude, the greater the energy contained in the wave.

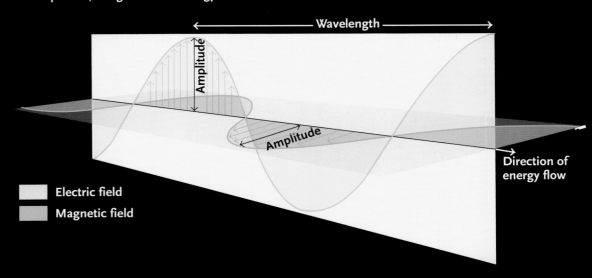

Wavelength

Amplitude

Amplitude

Direction of energy flow

Electric field
Magnetic field

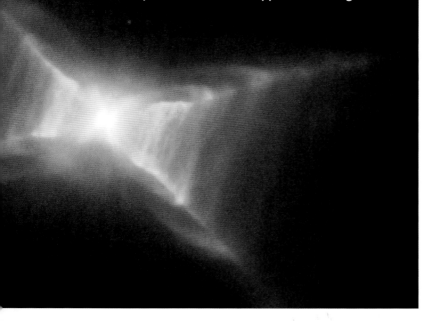

Ladder-like rungs and an X shape give a nebula called HD 44179 its informal name, the "Red Rectangle." Astronomers speculate that a thick cloud of dust surrounding the central stars in the nebula "pinches" the light emitted by the star into cone-shaped formations that appear as rectangles.

LIGHT'S LONG STRETCH

Light also becomes redshifted because of the expansion of space itself. This stretching is called cosmological redshift. Scientists believe that the universe began about 13.7 billion years ago in an explosion called the **big bang.** Since the big bang, the universe has expanded from a single point to its present size. As the universe expands, it stretches the light traveling through space. By measuring cosmological redshift, astronomers can tell how far away objects are. Light from the most distant galaxies shows the strongest redshift. Visible light from these objects has been stretched so much that it arrives as infrared light or **radio waves.**

DID YOU KNOW?

Photons, the particles that make up light, have energy but no mass or electric charge.

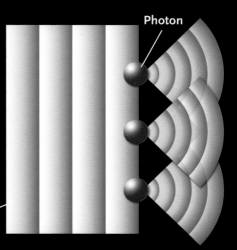

Although light travels in the form of waves, it is made of individual particles called photons.

Photon

Light waves

HUNGRY CORES

Some galaxies have centers that give off a tremendous amount of energy. Astronomers think that most galaxies have a large black hole lurking in their centers. Black holes are regions of space where gravity is so strong that nothing, not even light, can escape its pull. Some of these central black holes give off incredible amounts of energy. Part of the material spiraling in toward the black holes is converted into powerful jets of energy that can be seen from Earth.

Because AGN's are so far away, astronomers think they occurred only in the early universe. Scientists believe these early black holes are responsible for a group of galaxies that includes quasar, blazar, and radio galaxies. As a group, these galaxies are called active galactic nuclei (AGN's). AGN galaxies give off more electromagnetic energy over a longer period than any other source in the universe. Scientists believe that quasars are the most powerful of all AGN's.

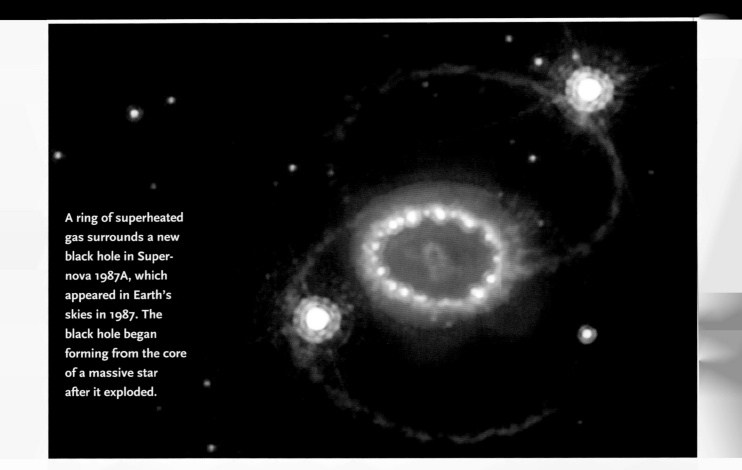

A ring of superheated gas surrounds a new black hole in Super-nova 1987A, which appeared in Earth's skies in 1987. The black hole began forming from the core of a massive star after it exploded.

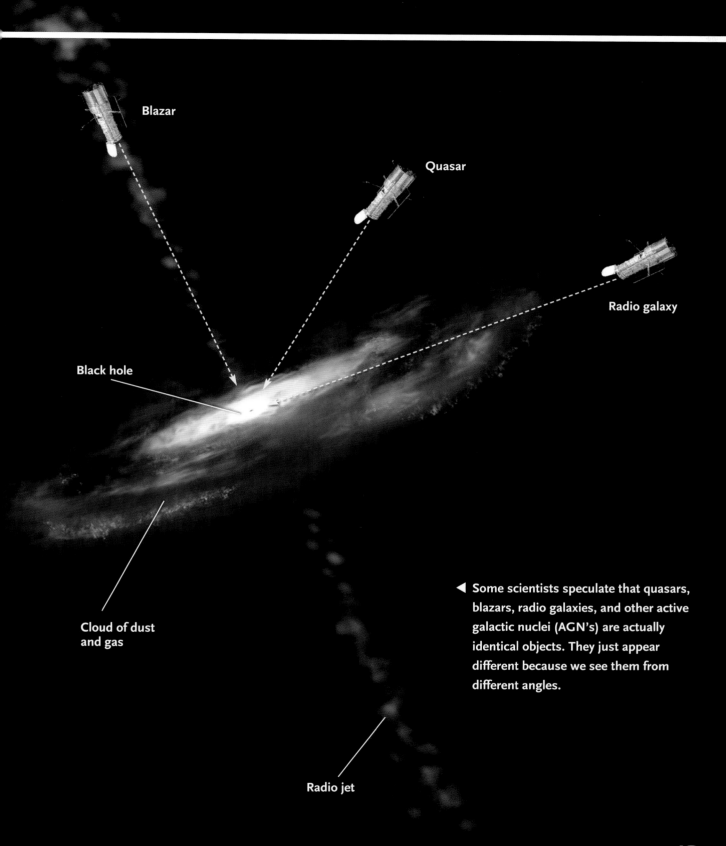

Blazar

Quasar

Radio galaxy

Black hole

Cloud of dust
and gas

◀ Some scientists speculate that quasars,
blazars, radio galaxies, and other active
galactic nuclei (AGN's) are actually
identical objects. They just appear
different because we see them from
different angles.

Radio jet

The Universe—Mysteries and Marvels   19

IS SPACE A TOTAL VACUUM?

IS THERE REALLY NOTHING?

Scientists have discovered that no space is ever truly empty. This knowledge comes from quantum mechanics, a branch of physics that describes the behavior of atoms and *subatomic particles* (pieces of matter smaller than atoms). According to the principles of quantum mechanics, particles can appear from nowhere as long as they disappear again in a sufficiently short time. Such particles are known as virtual particles. These particles give even empty space some energy, called vacuum energy.

MATTER IS EVERYWHERE

A vacuum holds far fewer molecules than the same volume of air at atmospheric pressures found near Earth's surface. One cubic centimeter of air at these pressures and room temperature has roughly 25 billion billion molecules on average. The best artificial vacuums on Earth contain an average of less than 1,000 molecules per cubic centimeter. Interstellar space, the space between the star systems, has an average of only about 1 atom per cubic centimeter.

A remarkable absence of celestial objects marks a region of the universe called Deep 3 Field, shown in a composite image of 74 frames taken by the Wide-Field Camera at the La Silla Observatory in Chile. The image reveals only about 50 galaxies or other objects in an area billions of light-years across.

WHERE IS THE MATTER?

Every part of the universe has at least a small amount of matter.

In the space between planets in the solar system (1), there is a constant flow of particles from the sun, bits of rock, and gas. In the spaces between stars in the Milky Way (2), the amount of matter decreases but remains relatively thick because gravity from galaxies keeps gas and dust nearby. As a result, the relatively empty space between galaxies (3) has only a thin layer of matter.

1
10 million atoms
per cubic meter
on average

2
10,000 atoms
per cubic meter
on average

3
1 atom
per cubic meter
on average

IN THE BEGINNING

The **big bang** theory ranks as the most widely accepted scientific theory about the origin of the universe. According to this theory, the universe once existed as a single point in space. The laws of physics do not provide a clear picture of how matter and energy behaved under the extreme heat and pressure at the instant of the big bang. Immediately after the explosion, the universe consisted chiefly of intense radiation and hot particles called **quarks.** This radiation, along with various kinds of matter and energy, formed a rapidly expanding region called the primordial fireball.

DID YOU KNOW?

The big bang theory was originally known as the thesis of the primeval atom. British astronomer Fred Hoyle, who had developed a different theory for the origin of the universe, first used the term "big bang" to refer to the explosion that began the expansion of the universe, and the name became widely used.

Most scientists believe that the universe began 13.7 billion years ago in an explosion called the big bang. The first stars formed about 200 million years later.

Oldest light

Big bang

Galaxies begin to form

First stars emit light, about 200 million years after the big bang

THE FIRST BUILDING BLOCKS

As the universe grew cooler and bigger, quarks joined together to make larger particles called *protons* (positively charged particles) and *neutrons* (particles with no electric charge). Within the first minutes after the big bang, the temperature of the universe had dropped to less than 1.8 billion °F

(1 billion °C). This was cool enough to allow protons and neutrons to join together to make objects that became the *nuclei* (centers) of atoms.

It took 380,000 years for the temperature to cool down to about 5,400 °F (3,000 °C). The atomic nuclei could then attract and hold negatively charged particles called electrons. One or more electrons orbiting around a nucleus form an atom, the smallest unit of a **chemical element.** Matter did not condense into **galaxies** for several hundred million years.

THE REMAINS OF THE BIG BANG

Evidence for the big bang theory comes partly from observations of the **cosmic microwave background (CMB) radiation,** energy from the early universe. The CMB radiation formed in the heat of the early universe and cooled as the universe expanded.

Scientists wondered why the CMB radiation appears smooth—that is, why its temperature is nearly the same in all directions. They also pondered how the universe's "clumpy" structure of galaxies and voids could arise from such apparent smoothness. To help explain these mysteries, physicists developed a theory called **inflation theory.** According to this theory, the universe expanded at an accelerated pace for a fraction of a second after the big bang. In addition, several space probes have found slight temperature variations in the CMB radiation. Scientists think the variations show that matter began to clump in the early universe. Over billions of years, the clumps grew into the galaxies that we can observe today.

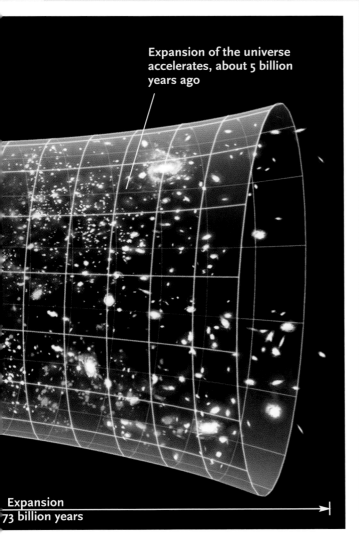

Expansion of the universe accelerates, about 5 billion years ago

Expansion
73 billion years

WHAT EXISTED BEFORE THE BIG BANG?

WAS THERE A BEFORE?

There is currently no way to observe or gather evidence that could give us any idea of what came before this colossal event. Was the **big bang** the beginning of the universe, or was it just another part of an endless cycle of expansion and contraction? There are many opinions about what came before this event.

THE BIRTH OF THE UNIVERSE

Some scientists speculate that nothing came before the big bang. They suggest that it marked the beginning of matter, space, and time. Other scientists theorize that the big bang marked the beginning of yet another episode of expansion and collapse—just one of many in a series of such events that goes on forever.

A theory sometimes known as "the big bounce" suggests that the universe expands and contracts in a repeating cycle. According to this theory, a universe similar to ours existed before the big bang. After a period of expansion, that previous universe began to shrink. When it shrank to a point smaller than an atom, it exploded into the current universe in the big bang.

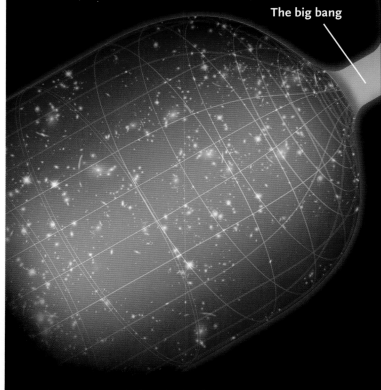

The big bang

Previous universe before the big bang

DID YOU KNOW?

As recently as the early 1900's, most scientists thought the Milky Way was the only galaxy in the universe. Today, scientists know there may be trillions of galaxies.

We can only guess what
existed before the big bang.

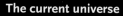

The current universe

Some scientists believe our universe began with the collision of two of the many universes that exist in space. This collision produced huge amounts of energy and matter that created our universe.

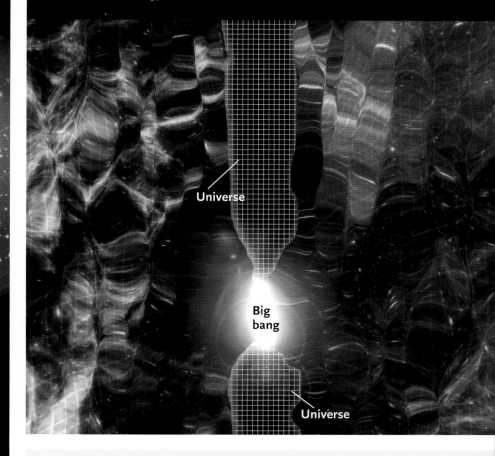

Universe

Big bang

Universe

ONE OF MANY

Still another line of thought suggests that the space we call our universe is just one of many. Other universes may be spread out across what has been called the multiverse, a larger eternal space with many universes. Perhaps our universe came into existence because of a collision between two of these universes.

WHAT IS THE COSMIC BACKGROUND RADIATION?

THE OLDEST LIGHT

After the event known as the **big bang,** the universe expanded and cooled. For a long time, it was too hot for atoms of matter to form. *Protons* (positively charged particles) and *electrons* (negatively charged particles) were present but had not yet come together to form atoms. **Photons** (particles of light) were also present, but they could not travel more than a brief distance before interacting with free electrons. As a result, the universe was a dense, foggy place.

Slight temperature variations in the cosmic microwave background (CMB) radiation are evident in a map of the universe created using data from the Wilkinson Microwave Anisotropy Probe (WMAP) satellite. Scientists think the variations show that matter began to clump in the early universe. Over billions of years, the clumps grew into the galaxies that are observed today.

The Planck microwave telescope, launched in 2009, was designed to produce the most detailed map yet of the CMB radiation.

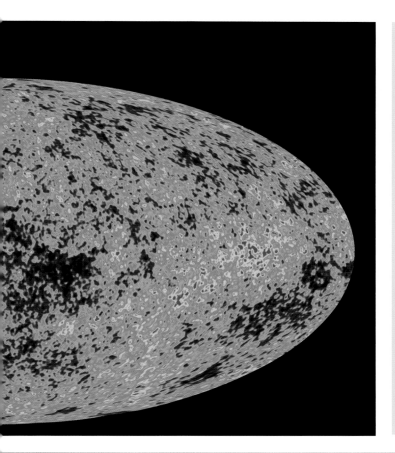

Around 380,000 years after the big bang, the temperature of the universe decreased enough for protons and electrons to combine into atoms. With most electrons bound into atoms, photons were able to penetrate space and carry light across the universe. A form of energy we call the **cosmic microwave background (CMB) radiation** represents the original light released after the formation of the first atoms. This light had much shorter **wavelengths** (the distance between the top of one wave and the next) than the CMB radiation observed today. However, over billions of years, the light has been stretched into **microwaves** by the expansion of space.

One of the first images of the CMB radiation from Planck, super-imposed on a photograph of the Milky Way, is nearly as detailed as images gathered by the WMAP project over five years. Planck images are expected to become even more detailed as the probe continues to scan the CMB radiation. (Solid red sections in the image represent microwave interference from the Milky Way.)

The Universe—Mysteries and Marvels   **27**

IS THE UNIVERSE EXPANDING?

HUBBLE'S SURPRISE

American astronomer Edwin Hubble noted in the early 1900's that **galaxies** were actually moving away from one another. He also realized that the farther away the galaxy was, the faster it was moving. These findings led astronomers to conclude that the universe has been expanding ever since it came into existence.

POINT OF NO RETURN

Scientists used to think that the expansion of the universe was slowing down. They believed that **gravity** from all the matter in the universe should cause this to happen. This led some scientists to predict that the universe would eventually reach a point where its expansion would stop and then reverse. This theory, called the "big crunch," is still debated. However, many scientists are now convinced that the universe will continue to expand forever. In fact, scientists have found evidence that the universe is actually expanding at an increasing rate. They have theorized that a mysterious force called **dark energy** is responsible. So far, scientists know very little about dark energy.

During the 1990's, scientists used the light from supernovae to determine that the expansion of the universe is accelerating. The increase in the rate of expansion is shown in the graph. The mysterious force causing this increase is called dark energy.

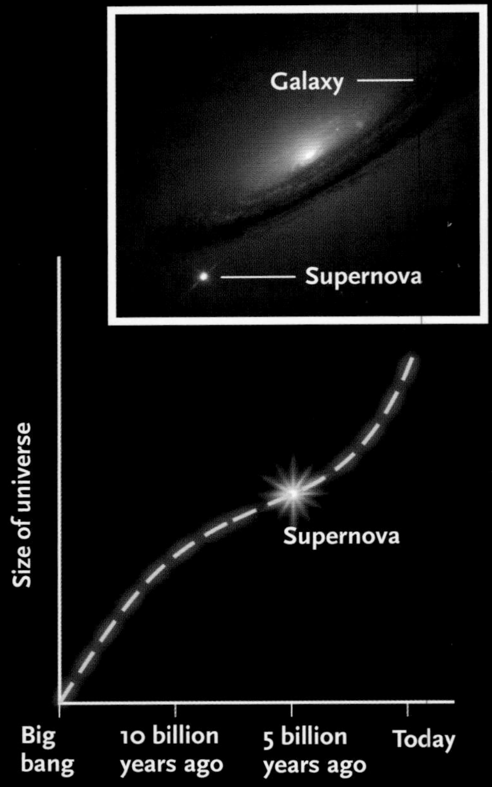

Galaxy

Supernova

Size of universe

Supernova

Big bang | 10 billion years ago | 5 billion years ago | Today

The Hubble telescope has produced images of some of the farthest galaxies in the universe. Edwin Hubble, the telescope's namesake, discovered that the farther the galaxy is from Earth, the faster it is moving away from Earth.

THREE POSSIBLE FUTURES

Until scientists determine the nature of dark energy, the future of the universe will remain uncertain. Depending on the actual nature of dark energy, the universe has at least three possible—and very different—futures.

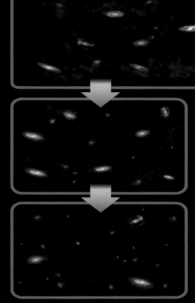

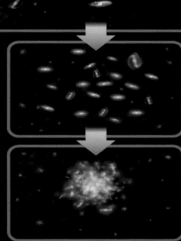

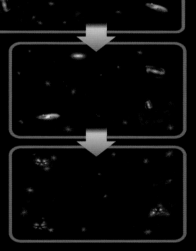

CONSTANT DARK ENERGY

If the density of dark energy remains the same (above), the expansion of the universe will accelerate at a constant rate, and galaxies will be pushed farther and farther apart. Within about 100 billion years, few other galaxies would be visible from our Milky Way.

BIG CRUNCH

If the density of dark energy decreases sufficiently (above), gravity will pull all galaxies back together in a "big crunch" within about 100 billion years. The universe could then experience another big bang.

BIG RIP

If the density of dark energy increases (above), the expansion of the universe will accelerate at an ever-increasing rate. Within about 50 billion years, every galaxy will be torn apart in a "big rip." According to this scenario, even atoms themselves would rip apart.

WHAT IS THE UNIVERSE EXPANDING INTO?

GROWING UNIVERSE

When the **big bang** occurred, the event was not just an explosion of energy and matter into the emptiness of space. It was also an explosion of space itself. So when we say that the universe is expanding, it actually means that space itself is expanding. For example, the distance between **galaxies** is growing not because they are moving in relation to each other but because the space between them is growing.

THE EXPANDING UNIVERSE

The big bang

After the big bang, the universe began to expand. The distances between stars, galaxies, and other objects grew as space expanded. Scientists can measure the expansion of space, called cosmological redshift, by observing the effect it has on light waves. As space expands, it stretches the light traveling through it. By measuring the amount of stretching, called redshift, scientists can estimate the rate of expansion.

Tycho's supernova remnant (above) and other celestial objects are moving away from us faster than scientists had previously believed. In the 1990's, astronomers studying supernovae, like the one that created this remnant, discovered that light from the supernovae was redshifted more than expected. This high amount of redshift showed that the supernovae were moving away from us faster than we previously thought. Because of this observation, astronomers now believe the expansion of the universe is accelerating.

DID YOU KNOW?

The estimated temperature of the universe one second after the big bang was from 1 billion to 100 billion Kelvin (1.7 billion to 180 billion °F).

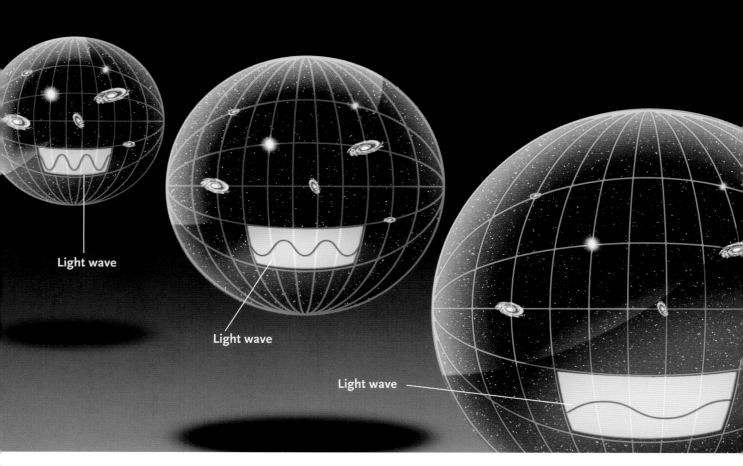

Light wave

Light wave

Light wave

PULLED ALONG FOR THE RIDE

A good way to understand how the universe expands is to compare it with raisin bread dough as it rises. The dough itself represents the universe, and the raisins are galaxies. As the dough expands, the raisins move farther apart. The raisins don't actually move through the dough; they are moved along with the dough. Similarly, the universe expands and pushes galaxies apart. Because it is the universe itself that is expanding, there is nothing outside the universe for the universe to expand into.

WHAT ARE HIGH-ENERGY COSMIC RAYS?

POWERHOUSE PARTICLES

Since the early 1900's, researchers have been aware of the existence of **cosmic rays**. Unlike **electromagnetic radiation,** which consists of **photons,** cosmic rays consist of *subatomic particles* (particles smaller than an atom). These particles, which include electrons, protons, and atomic nuclei, are much more massive. Because of their **mass** (amount of matter), these particles contain tremendous amounts of energy. So far, no one knows for sure where cosmic rays come from. But scientists have several theories about their origins.

Cosmic rays are the only known matter that reaches Earth from outside the solar system. They may spend millions of years traveling through space before arriving on Earth. An estimated 200 cosmic-ray particles strike every square yard on Earth every second.

The Pierre Auger Observatory in Argentina uses 1,600 cosmic-ray detectors spread out over an area the size of the state of Rhode Island.

MYSTERIOUS ORIGINS

Scientists are fairly certain that the lowest-energy cosmic rays come from **supernovae** in our galaxy. However, some cosmic rays have too much energy to have come from even supernovae. Scientists suspect that the highest-energy cosmic rays may originate in **quasars.** These objects release more energy than any other objects in the universe. Whatever the origin of cosmic rays, when they enter Earth's atmosphere, they interact with particles there and produce a "shower" of secondary particles.

Several observatories, including the Pierre Auger Observatory in Argentina, are being used to study these high-energy rays. Scientists hope that these strange particles will one day reveal information about the most extreme parts of the universe.

Cosmic rays entering Earth's atmosphere collide with gas molecules, producing an avalanche of secondary particles. The first of these particles, called pions, exist for only a few billionths of a second before breaking down into a variety of subatomic particles. The heaviest of these, called muons, reach the surface and may even penetrate thousands of meters below the surface.

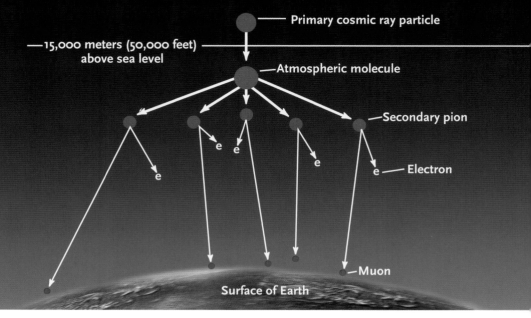

Primary cosmic ray particle

15,000 meters (50,000 feet) above sea level

Atmospheric molecule

Secondary pion

Electron

Muon

Surface of Earth

GAMMA-RAY BURSTS— OUTSHINING THE UNIVERSE

When the universe was still much younger and much smaller, some stars grew larger than anything astronomers see today. These stars were so large that some scientists use the term *hypernova* to describe the violent explosion that marked the end of their life.

Hypernovae are seen in distant, ancient regions of the universe. Many astronomers believe that hypernovae are the sources of gamma-ray bursts (GBR's), pulses of the most energetic form of electromagnetic energy. These bursts are thousands of times as energetic as the largest supernovae. This suggests that the events that caused the gamma-ray bursts were far stronger than the supernovae we see closer to Earth today.

Powerful jets of gamma rays shoot from a galaxy after a gamma-ray burst that occurred in 2005, shown in an artist's illustration. The GRB, located about 2 billion light-years away, lasted only half a second. Because it occurred near the edge of a galaxy, astronomers concluded that it was likely the result of a collision between two neutron stars or a neutron star and a black hole.

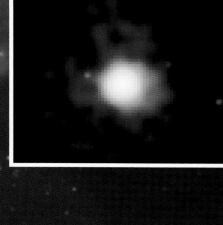

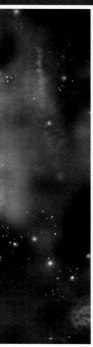

One type of gamma-ray burst called a dark burst (center) gives off gamma rays and X rays but no visible light. Recent studies suggest that thick clouds of gas and dust, shown in green, block the visible light coming from the burst.

The gamma-ray burst GRB 080319B (shown in an artist's illustration) was 2,500 times as powerful as the most powerful supernova ever recorded. Observed in early 2008 (inset), GRB 080319B could be seen with the unaided eye even though it was about 7.5 billion light-years away.

ANTIGRAVITY

In the late 1990's, astronomers determined that the universe is not just expanding; the rate of expansion is speeding up. Something must be making this happen. The term **dark energy** is used to describe this mysterious force. Dark energy seems to oppose the force of **gravity.** Rather than pulling objects closer together, dark energy pushes them apart. The more the universe expands, the more dark energy there seems to be. Measurements indicate that the density of dark energy throughout the universe is greater than the density of matter.

"INVISIBLE" ENERGY

Although astronomers are relatively sure that dark energy is present in the universe, they don't yet understand it— what it's made of or what causes it. Further study of this curious form of energy will help us better understand the future of the universe.

DID YOU KNOW?

Because dark energy is not affected by gravity, it is the only thing in the universe that could avoid being pulled into a black hole.

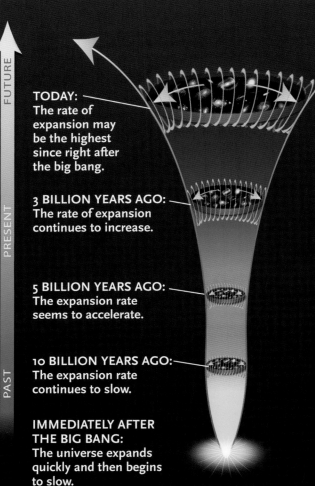

TODAY:
The rate of expansion may be the highest since right after the big bang.

3 BILLION YEARS AGO:
The rate of expansion continues to increase.

5 BILLION YEARS AGO:
The expansion rate seems to accelerate.

10 BILLION YEARS AGO:
The expansion rate continues to slow.

IMMEDIATELY AFTER THE BIG BANG:
The universe expands quickly and then begins to slow.

BIG BANG

FUTURE · PRESENT · PAST

Dark energy and an invisible form of matter called dark matter influence the rate at which the universe is expanding. Dark energy seems to *repel* (push apart) visible matter, and dark matter seems to *constrain* it (pull it together) by its gravity. About 5 billion years ago, the repelling force of dark energy became more powerful than the constraining gravity of dark matter and ordinary matter. At this point the universe began to expand at an *accelerated* (faster) rate.

Dark energy is an unknown form of energy thought to be accelerating the expansion of the universe.

The Abell 85 galaxy cluster (purple) is one of 86 galaxy clusters under the observation of the Chandra X-ray Observatory. These observations are trying to trace how dark energy has slowed the growth of these structures over the last 7 billion years.

AN EARLY BATTLE

Scientists think that both matter and **antimatter** formed in the first microseconds after the **big bang.** Like matter, antimatter is made up of elementary particles—that is, particles with no smaller parts. However, certain properties of antimatter elementary particles are the opposite of their matter "twins."

When matter and antimatter meet, they destroy each other, leaving nothing but energy. However, in the first moments after the big bang, matter and antimatter were also created from energy. Energy, matter, and antimatter were continually being created and destroyed in the early universe. Scientists think that these particles rapidly switched back and forth between matter and energy until settling into a fixed form.

The physical universe changed rapidly in the first billionth of a second after the big bang. Gravity separated from what had been one united force and became the first of the four basic forces of nature. The other forces—the strong nuclear force, the weak nuclear force, and electromagnetism—separated soon afterward. Within a few seconds, one form of matter called antimatter virtually disappeared, leaving ordinary matter to form into the simplest atomic nuclei. After a period of expansion and cooling, protons and electrons formed full atoms around 380,000 years later.

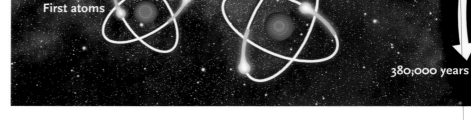

United force

Antimatter is destroyed, leaving matter

Smallest subatomic particles of matter begin to combine

Protons, electrons and neutrons

Atomic nuclei

First atoms

1 second

380,000 years

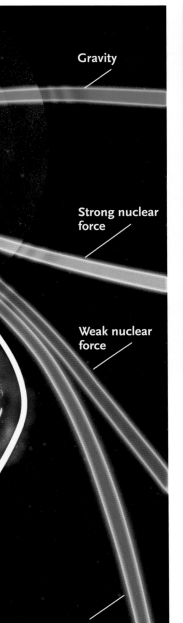

Gravity

Strong nuclear force

Weak nuclear force

Electromagnetism

ATOM OF MATTER

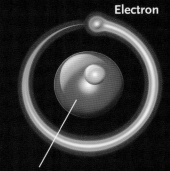

Electron

Nucleus made of a proton or a proton and neutron

ATOM OF ANTIMATTER

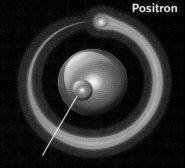

Positron

Nucleus made of an antiproton or an antiproton and antineutron

Antimatter and matter are mirror images of each other. The particles that make up atoms—electrons, protons, and neutrons—all have antimatter "opposites." Scientists are unsure why more matter than antimatter was created in the big bang.

SOME THINGS REALLY MATTER

Today there is far more matter than antimatter. This situation presents a problem for scientists. If matter and antimatter were created in equal amounts right after the big bang, they should have totally annihilated each other. The universe would be filled only with energy. Something happened to give matter the edge over antimatter. Physicists have calculated that it would have taken only one more particle per billion particles of matter compared with antimatter to create the matter-filled universe that we see today.

Matter is the building block of anything we can see and touch—including **planets, stars,** animals, and plants. People are also a product of that moment when a phenomenal event caused matter to come into existence.

WHAT IS DARK MATTER?

A SERIOUS MATTER

Stars, planets, galaxies, and everything else we can see make up one-sixth or less of what is out there in our universe. We know that something more exists, because that "something" has **gravity.** But strangely, this matter doesn't give off or reflect radiation as ordinary matter does. Scientists call this mysterious substance **dark matter.**

Images of one section of the sky at different times in the past, taken by the Hubble Space Telescope, have enabled astronomers to construct a three-dimensional map of the dark matter in that area. They determined the location of the dark matter by observing how its gravity affected the objects and light nearby.

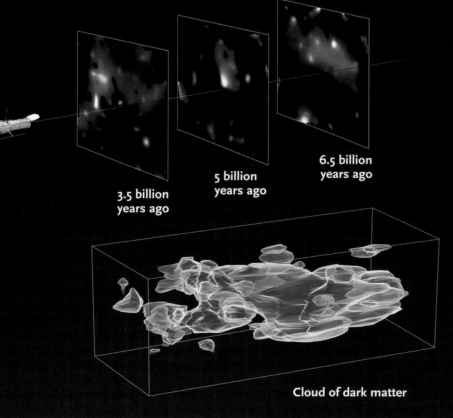

3.5 billion years ago

5 billion years ago

6.5 billion years ago

Cloud of dark matter

Clouds of dark matter (colorized in blue) surround a massive galaxy cluster (colorized in pink) that formed from the collision of two galaxy clusters, in a composite image made using data from the Hubble Space Telescope and Chandra X-ray Observatory. The collision slowed the visible matter in the clusters but not the surrounding dark matter.

The types of matter and energy that make up the universe have changed since the big bang 13.7 billion years ago. The early universe contained a large proportion of dark matter as well as *photons* (light particles), atoms, and neutrinos. Today, dark energy and dark matter dominate the universe.

INVISIBLE GALACTIC GLUE

There are several clues to the nature of dark matter. For example, astronomers found that **galaxies** were rotating faster than expected given their observed *mass* (amount of matter). In fact, this rotation was so fast that they should have flown apart. Stronger gravity from invisible matter had to be holding them together. Dark matter is thought to be the source.

Another clue involves **galaxy clusters,** which hold hot intergalactic gas. The gas is so hot, it should escape from the area of space in which it's located. Instead, it stays put. Scientists believe that the gravity of dark matter keeps it from escaping.

Many scientists think it likely that dark matter is made up of huge numbers of subatomic particles. Scientists are busily trying to identify these particles. Dark matter remains one of the most important puzzles remaining in astronomy today.

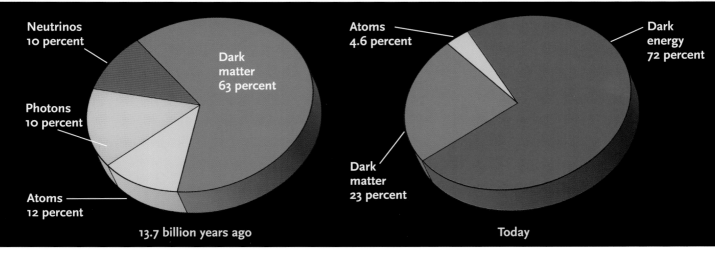

Neutrinos 10 percent

Photons 10 percent

Atoms 12 percent

Dark matter 63 percent

13.7 billion years ago

Atoms 4.6 percent

Dark energy 72 percent

Dark matter 23 percent

Today

WHAT DO WE KNOW ABOUT BLACK HOLES?

An unusual black hole (upper left) captures gas being shed by a companion star (right) in an artist's illustration. The two objects are referred to as the IC 10 X-1 system. Unlike supermassive black holes, the black hole in the IC 10 X-1 system does not occupy the center of a galaxy. One of the largest known "stellar-mass" black holes, it formed as a massive star collapsed.

UNMATCHED GRAVITY

A **black hole** begins as a supermassive **star** with gravity so strong that it collapses on itself. The remaining core continues to compress, forming an invisible center. As a black hole continues to attract more and more matter, its **mass** increases, creating an ever-growing gravitational pull.

OBSERVING THE INVISIBLE

The structure of a black hole consists of the **accretion disk**, the swirling whirlpool of matter that orbits the black hole; the **event horizon,** the "edge" of the black hole, where matter becomes trapped; and the **singularity,** the actual center of the black hole, where all matter ends up.

Black holes are objects with such strong gravity, nothing passing nearby can escape, not even light.

A black hole is a hole in the "fabric" of space. Anything moving too close to it, even light, will fall down the slope of the hole into the center, never to escape.

NOT SO RARE

There are more black holes in the universe than once thought. The Milky Way alone may contain millions of black holes. In the past several years, scientists have determined that a supermassive black hole sits at the center of most galaxies, including our own.

Because black holes are a rather strange discovery with unusual properties, they have fascinated scientists and nonscientists alike. Some think that black holes could become gateways to other universes.

The black hole at the center of the Milky Way (arrow) is known as Sagittarius A*. Black holes are invisible because they trap light. However, they heat the gas cloud surrounding them, allowing astronomers to determine their location.

MAKING BLACK HOLES?

The **micro black holes** predicted by scientists are so tiny that each one would be the size of an atom. Compared with their size, their *mass* (amount of matter) would be huge—equal to that of a large mountain on Earth.

British physicist Stephen Hawking first predicted the existence of micro black holes. He believes that they might have developed immediately after the **big bang.**

Due to the incredibly hot temperatures of the universe at that time, small bits of matter might have been pressed together, causing extremely intense **gravity.**

Some scientists have predicted that a powerful particle accelerator could prduce micro black holes. Even if this were possible, the black holes would last for only a brief instant, posing no threat to the machine or to people.

The **Large Hadron Collider (LHC)** is the largest scientific experiment ever created. The underground accelerator tunnel (shown in outline) is about 17 miles (27 kilometers) in circumference.

Subatomic particles are created in a computer simulation of a high-speed collision in a particle accelerator like the LHC.

Even if the Large Hadron Collider could produce micro black holes, these objects would vanish almost instantly and pose no threat to the machine or to people.

DID YOU KNOW?

At full intensity, the Large Hadron Collider will produce 600 million collisions per second.

NOT ALONE

In the 1990's, scientists located the first orbiting **planets** outside the **solar system.** As of the end of 2009, more than 400 other planets had been found rotating around distant stars. Many of these **planetary systems** are quite different from our own.

NEEDLE IN A HAYSTACK

Other planetary systems are very difficult to locate. The **stars** of these planetary systems outshine the planets, making it almost impossible to detect the faint reflected light of any planet. Astronomers have had more success by looking for stars that "wobble" because they are being tugged by the **gravity** of their planets.

Scientists believe that we will soon find worlds similar to Earth as new, more-powerful telescopes become available. Eventually, this effort may even lead to the discovery of alien life.

Three of the four planets known to orbit the dim, red dwarf star Gliese 581, are shown in an artist's illustration. One of the planets orbits in the star's habitable zone, the area around the star in which a planet may contain liquid water.

Astronomers have discovered planets orbiting around other stars. These other systems are known as planetary systems.

The extrasolar planet HD 70642b, which is about twice as massive as Jupiter, dominates the sky above a hypothetical moon in an artist's illustration. The planet's orbit is about 3/5 of the distance from its star as Jupiter is from the sun. This suggests that smaller, possibly Earth-like planets might also be a part of this planetary system.

IS THERE LIFE IN OTHER PARTS OF THE UNIVERSE?

ANYONE HOME?

For generations, the question of whether there is **extraterrestrial life,** or life on other **planets,** has fascinated scientists and nonscientists alike. Not that long ago, efforts to search for other life in the universe were not considered serious science. But things are changing.

IS THERE ANOTHER EARTH?

Many scientists have devoted their careers to determining what it takes for life to evolve in the universe. They study the conditions on Earth and speculate about other places in the universe that might have these same conditions. The fact that there are so many **stars** in the universe makes them feel quite certain that Earth could not be the only place where the right conditions for life exist.

LISTENING FOR A SIGN

American astronomer Frank Drake is considered to be the first person to come up with a scientific formula for determining the probability of extraterrestrial life. He conducted his research at the SETI Institute in California. SETI stands for "Search for Extraterrestrial Intelligence." Here, giant radio telescopes pan the skies, searching for signals created by other civilizations. Drake calculated that the Milky Way Galaxy alone could have 10,000 detectable civilizations.

Plumes of gas and ice particles are ejected into space from Saturn's moon Enceladus. Many scientists agree that the moon may have a layer of liquid water somewhere below its icy surface. Water is essential for life as we know it.

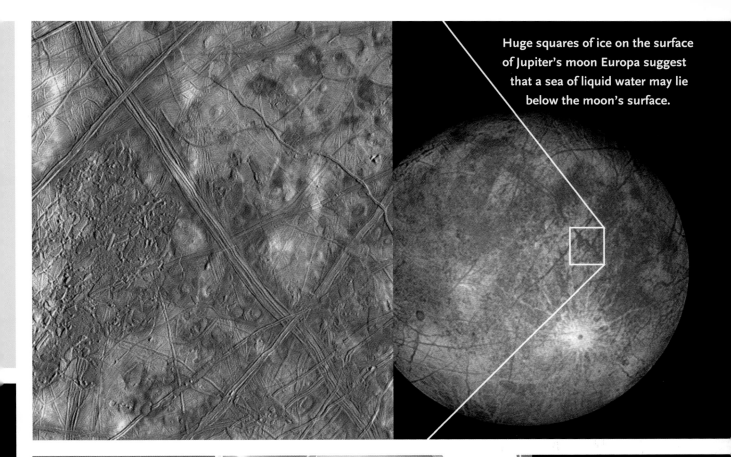

Huge squares of ice on the surface of Jupiter's moon Europa suggest that a sea of liquid water may lie below the moon's surface.

The Allen Telescope Array, operated by the SETI Institute in California, is the only large telescope dedicated to the search for extraterrestrial life. The radio telescope has 47 dishes that work as one big instrument to listen for signals made by extraterrestrial technology.

THE UNIVERSE'S LARGEST MAGNETS

When a star reaches the end of its life, it usually "dies" in one of two ways. It may burn down slowly or it may explode in a massive release of energy called a supernova.

When a star a few times larger than the sun begins to run out of fuel, drastic changes begin, eventually leading to a supernova. But this massive explosion is not the complete end of the star.

Really large stars collapse into a tiny yet massive region of space called a black hole. Slightly smaller stars may become a very dense and highly magnetic object called a neutron star. These stars can spin at rates of many times a second. One type of neutron star, called a pulsar, emits a beacon of high-energy light that flashes like the beam of a lighthouse. Still another type of neutron star, called a magnetar, has a magnetic field over a trillion times as strong as that of the sun.

A magnetic field is the influence that a magnetic object creates in the region around it. Scientists think that in some cases, disturbances called starquakes can crack the magnetar's crust, producing severe disruptions in the star's magnetic field. The rapidly changing magnetic field can generate powerful bursts of X rays and gamma rays. The main distinction between a pulsar and a magnetar is the source of their power. The power of a pulsar comes from its rapid spin, but a magnetar's power comes from its tremendously strong magnetic field.

◄ The first magnetar discovered by astronomers outshines the bright swirls of gas and dust in which it was born. Astronomers realized that they were observing a new type of star when several space probes registered intense blasts of gamma rays coming from a point in the Large Magellanic Cloud on March 5, 1979. The magnetar, pinpointed as the source of the blasts, formed in the remnants of a supernova whose light reached Earth thousands of years ago.

A magnetar can produce jets of energy (large white lines) much like its neutron star cousin, the pulsar. However, the power behind the magnetar's jets comes from the extremely strong magnetic field (blue lines) produced by the magnetar. On the other hand, a pulsar gains its power from its rapid spin. Both objects are neutron stars, the extremely dense core that remains after a star has exploded in a supernova.

COULD THE UNIVERSE BE MADE OF STRINGS?

STRINGY PARTICLES

Some scientists believe that the elementary particles that make up all matter consist of unimaginably weird, thread-like loops of energy called superstrings, or strings for short. If you could see these strings, they would appear to be vibrating, merging, breaking apart, disappearing,

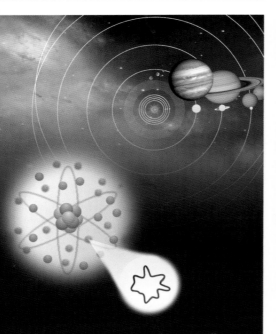

In size, a superstring theoretically compares with an atom the way an atom compares with our solar system.

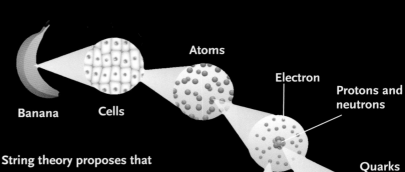

String theory proposes that tiny loops of energy called superstrings are the most basic unit of matter and force in the universe.

The atoms that make up an object, such as a banana, are themselves made up of many subatomic particles. Protons and neutrons form an atom's *nucleus* (core), which is surrounded by electrons. Quarks form protons and neutrons.

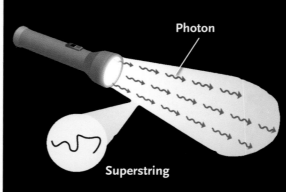

String theory also proposes that the particles that transmit forces are made of strings. For example, wave-like particles called photons transmit the electromagnetic force, which includes visible light. Accordingly, photons themselves are made of strings.

According to one scientific theory, the universe could consist of incredibly small loops of energy called strings.

Superstrings and the strings of musical instruments, such as guitars, have a lot in common, including elasticity, the ability to stretch and return to their original shape. However, superstrings don't need to be plucked like guitar strings; they can play themselves.

Each string on a guitar vibrates in a different way when plucked. The various patterns of the vibrations (below, left) determine the musical notes that the strings produce.

In a similar way, the vibration patterns of superstrings (right) determine the types of particles the superstrings give rise to. The more energetic the vibrations, the greater the mass of the particles. (Increasing energy is shown from top to bottom.)

Whether a superstring forms a closed loop (left, top) or has open ends (bottom) also influences what type of particle the superstring produces. For example, physicists theorize that *photons* (light particles) are made of open superstrings.

and reappearing right before your eyes. And they would be doing this in nine or more different dimensions of space, not just the three spatial dimensions we normally experience—height, width, and thickness (or depth). These ideas form the basis of **string theory.**

AN ELEGANT SOLUTION

To understand superstrings, it helps to think about the strings of a guitar. Both superstrings and guitar strings are elastic—able to stretch, vibrate, and then return to their original shape. A guitar string, when plucked, creates a pattern of vibrations that creates a musical note. But a superstring vibrates on its own. Its pattern of vibrations determines the type of particle it will become and what **mass** it will hold. According to string theory, strings are as small as anything theoretically could be. Physicists believe strings measure approximately 0.00000000000000000000000000000001 centimeter long.

String theory is a new way to think about everything in the universe. It helps scientists make connections between the behavior of all matter, whether gigantic or infinitely small. String theory also might help explain **dark matter,** the invisible and mysterious substance or substances thought to make up the majority of the matter in the universe.

INVISIBLE WORLDS

In recent years, scientists have suggested that there may be more dimensions than they had previously identified. The dimensions of an object are commonly described as height, width, and thickness (or depth). If additional dimensions exist, it's possible that other universes exist as well, totally undetected.

THE WORLDS NEXT DOOR

One idea is called **brane theory.** It proposes that the universe we can observe exists as a membrane, or a brane for short, within a larger, many-dimensional space. The brane that makes up the universe we know is only a thin slice. There might even be other branes. We may not be able to detect these branes because our instruments are limited.

Some scientists have taken this idea of the universe one step farther. They wonder if the **big bang** actually took place because our universe—or brane—intersected or collided with a neighboring brane.

Scientists theorize that we cannot see extra dimensions because the universe we live in exists on a membrane-like surface called a brane, or a "braneworld" (below). This brane is only a thin slice of the entire "megaverse" in which the extra dimensions lie. According to this idea, other universes on other branes also make thin slices through the multidimensional megaverse.

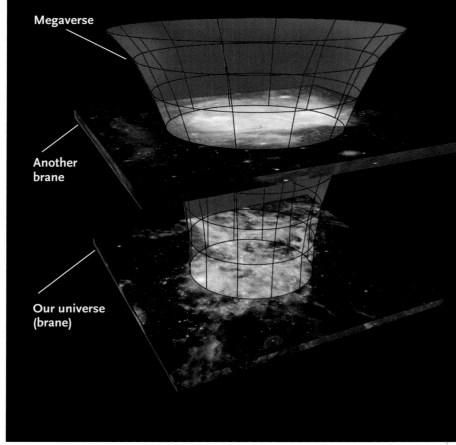

Megaverse

Another brane

Our universe (brane)

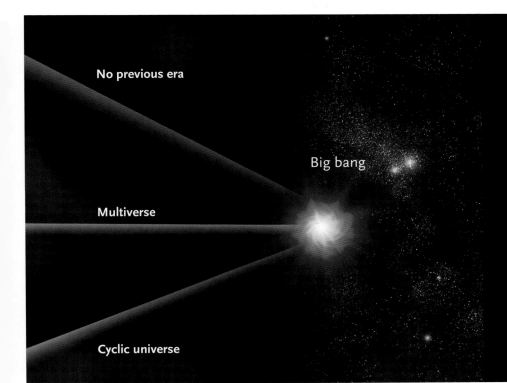

No previous era

Big bang

Multiverse

Cyclic universe

Most scientists agree that the big bang marked the beginning of the current universe. However, there is no current way to observe events before this event. Scientists have theorized (1) that nothing may have existed before the big bang; that (2) there may be many possible universes and that the big bang occurred when two of them touched; or that (3) our current universe may be just one in a repeating cycle of expansion, contraction, and big bangs.

LIFE IN EXTRA DIMENSIONS

Even in a world with just one extra dimension, you would find it very difficult to get back to your starting point once you had wandered away. You would see objects and people become dimmer, then vanish rapidly as you move away from them. This is because light would spread out and fade much more rapidly than in the "normal" world. By the same token, you would find it impossible to hear others unless you were right next to them, because sound also spreads out and fades rapidly.

THE FOURTH DIMENSION

We usually think of the world as consisting of three dimensions of space—length, width, and height. What we call *time* is really the changes we see in the three-dimensional world: spring turns to summer, the school year begins, we get older, and so on.

But time is a dimension, too. For example, if you planned to meet a friend at the mall, you would need four pieces of information. You would need to know whether your meeting place lies toward the north or south end of the mall and toward the east or west end of the mall. These two pieces of information represent the dimensions of length and width. You would also need to know on which floor of the mall you will be meeting. This information represents height. But even if you knew all these three dimensions of place, you could miss your friend if you did not know the fourth dimension—time.

In the early 1900's, physicist Albert Einstein proposed that time and space were more deeply connected than people previously thought.

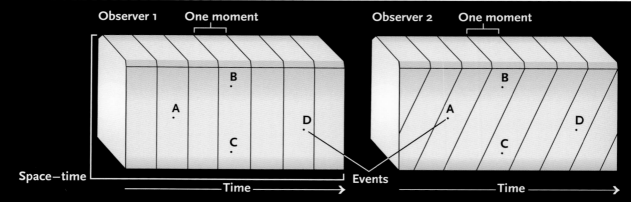

The experience of time in relativity in some ways resembles slicing a loaf of bread. The "loaf" represents all the events that occur throughout *space-time* (the combination of space and time). Each "slice" contains the events that happen at a single moment. Just as a loaf of bread can be sliced any number of ways, observers can experience space-time differently depending on their states of motion. For an observer in one state of motion, events B and C might occur at the same moment (above, left). An observer in another state of motion would experience the same events differently. For that observer, event B might occur before event C (above).

Although we don't usually think of it in this way, time is a dimension.

TIME IS SPACE?

In the early part of the 1900's, German-born American physicist Albert Einstein theorized that time is a dimension in itself and that it is inseparable from the three dimensions of space. Together, these dimensions make up **space-time.**

One of Einstein's findings was that the faster an object moves through space, the slower it moves through time. This is often explained with the example of twins. Let's say that one twin travels into space at near the speed of light. For her, time would move more slowly than it would for her twin brother back on Earth. When the space-traveling twin returned home, she would find that her brother would actually be older than she is. Scientists have confirmed this effect with experiments.

The Prague Orloj, an astronomical clock in Prague, Czech Republic, gives information on the sun, moon, stars, and seasons all on one face. It was built in 1410.

SKIPPING THROUGH TIME

For centuries, people have speculated about the possibility of traveling forward or backward in time. Science-fiction writers and filmmakers have imagined what time travel would be like. But in reality, the scientific world has not reached the point of knowing how time travel could take place. However, the theories of Albert Einstein suggest that time travel might one day be possible.

SHORTCUTS IN SPACE

Wormholes might allow time travel. Wormholes are "shortcuts" through **space-time.** Scientists and science-fiction writers imagine wormholes as tunnels connecting one area of space to another. A wormhole has two ends. Matter would enter through one hole and exit through the other. Some people have wondered whether wormholes could bridge two places, either within our own universe or in two different

Space-time

Wormhole

Ideas about wormholes are based on the theory of general relativity developed by the German-born American physicist Albert Einstein. According to this theory, matter curves space. Over vast distances, matter causes space to curve back on itself in the shape of the letter U. The short strip of space connecting the two "uprights" of the U would be a wormhole.

The vastness of the universe and the great distances between objects make traveling between them almost impossible. Unless we learn how to travel faster than the speed of light, the time it would take to get to any other star would be many times longer than our lifetime.

The Time Machine

H. G. Wells

The Time Machine by H. G. Wells, published in 1895, describes the adventures of a man who builds a machine that can transport him into the future. The novel became one of the most popular stories about time travel.

universes. A space ship would enter the wormhole. One model of a wormhole suggests that the ends of the wormhole spin at near the speed of light, slowing down time. If this were true, the space ship would leave the other end of the wormhole before it ever went in! Although they are fun to think about, scientists have found no proof that wormholes exist.

DID YOU KNOW?

Although the nature of time is mysterious, we can measure time more accurately than any other quantity.

GLOSSARY

Accretion disk — A disk-shaped formation of gases or other interstellar matter around a massive body such as a star.

Antimatter — A substance that resembles ordinary matter but with certain properties of its particles, such as electric charge, reversed.

Big bang — The cosmic explosion that began the expansion of the universe.

Black hole — The collapsed core of a massive star. The gravity of a black hole is so strong that not even light can escape.

Brane theory — The idea that the known universe is only a membrane within a larger, many-dimensional space.

Chemical element — Any substance that contains only one kind of atom. Hydrogen and helium are both chemical elements.

Cosmic microwave background (CMB) radiation — The most ancient electromagnetic radiation in the universe. Variations in the CMB radiation correspond to the distribution of galaxies in the universe today.

Cosmic rays — Electrically charged, high-energy particles that travel through space.

Dark energy — A mysterious form of energy that is causing the expansion of the universe to accelerate.

Dark matter — A mysterious form of matter that does not reflect or absorb light. The majority of matter in the universe is dark matter.

Doppler effect — The change in wavelength of light or sound caused by the relative motion of the source and the observer.

Electromagnetic radiation — Any form of light, ranging from radio waves, to microwaves, to infrared light, to visible light, to ultraviolet light, to X rays, to gamma rays.

Event horizon — The boundary of a black hole where the pull of gravity becomes stronger than any other force.

Extraterrestrial life — Life that originates beyond Earth.

Galaxy — A vast system of stars, gas, dust, and other matter held together in space by mutual gravitational attraction.

Galaxy cluster — A concentration of hundreds to thousands of galaxies held together by gravity.

Gamma rays — The form of light with the shortest wavelengths. Gamma rays are invisible to the unaided eye.

Gravity — The force of attraction that acts between all objects because of their mass.

Inflation theory — The theory, in physics, that the early universe experienced an extremely brief period of particularly rapid expansion.

Infrared light — A form of light with long wavelengths. Also called heat radiation. Infrared is invisible to the unaided eye.

Light-year — The distance light travels in a vacuum in one year. One light-year is equal to 5.88 trillion miles (9.46 trillion kilometers).

Luminosity — The rate at which an object gives off electromagnetic radiation. Apparent luminosity is the amount of this radiation that reaches the Earth.

Mass — The amount of matter in an object.

Micro black hole — A black hole with far less mass than a conventional black hole.

Microwaves — A kind of radio waves with relatively short wavelengths. Microwaves are invisible to the unaided eye.

Nebula — A cloud of dust and gas in space.

Optical — Of or relating to visible light.

Photon — The elementary particle that makes up all forms of electromagnetic radiation.

Planet — A large, round heavenly body that orbits a star.

Quark — An elementary subatomic particle that makes up the basic building blocks of matter.

Quasar — An extremely bright object at the center of some distant galaxies. Scientists believe quasars are powered by supermassive black holes.

Redshift — A shift in light's wavelength toward longer, redder wavelengths. Doppler redshift is caused by the Doppler effect. Cosmological redshift is caused by the expansion of the universe.

Radio waves — The form of light with the longest wavelengths. Radio waves are invisible to the unaided eye.

Singularity — The point at the center of a black hole where the core has collapsed to a space smaller than an atom.

Solar system — The planetary system that includes the sun and Earth.

Space-time — Space conceived as a continuum of four dimensions, namely length, width, height, and time. Physicist Albert Einstein's theories of relativity showed that space and time are fundamentally joined.

Spectrum, spectra — Light divided into its different wavelengths. A spectrum may provide astronomers with information about a heavenly body's chemical composition, motion, and distance.

Star — A huge, shining ball in space that produces a tremendous amount of visible light and other forms of energy.

String theory — A theory of the fundamental forces of nature. It proposes that the elementary particles that make up matter consist of incredibly tiny, vibrating strings.

Supernova, supernovae — An exploding star that can become billions of times as bright as the sun before gradually fading from view. A supernova occurs when a massive star uses up all its fuel.

Ultraviolet light — A form of light with short wavelengths. Ultraviolet light is invisible to the unaided eye.

Visible light — The form of light human beings can see with their eyes.

Wavelength — The distance between successive crests, or peaks, of a wave.

Weakly interacting massive particle (WIMP) — A theoretical, slow-moving particle thought to make up dark matter.

X rays — A form of light with very short wavelengths. X rays are invisible to the unaided eye.

FOR MORE INFORMATION

WEB SITES

Cosmicopia
http://helios.gsfc.nasa.gov
NASA's Astrophysics Science Division explains how the energy from atoms affects the sun's activities, cosmic rays, magnetic fields, dark matter, and other wonders of the universe.

First Galaxies
http://www.firstgalaxies.org
Learn what we know so far, and what astronomers may yet discover, about how the universe began and galaxies formed.

Science & Nature: Space
http://www.bbc.co.uk/science/space/
The British Broadcasting Company gives an overview of astronomy, covering such broad topics as the solar system and stars, and more complex topics, including deep space and theories about the origins of the universe.

SETI Institute
http://www.seti.org
SETI (Search for Extraterrestrial Intelligence) conducts research to see if there might be life elsewhere in the universe.

BOOKS

The Big Bang
by Paul Fleisher (Twenty-first Century Books, 2006)

Death Stars, Weird Galaxies, and a Quasar-Spangled Universe
by Karen Taschek (University of New Mexico Press, 2006)

Einstein's Telescope: The Hunt for Dark Matter and Dark Energy in the Universe by Evalyn Gates (Norton, 2009)

Mysterious Universe: Supernovae, Dark Energy, and Black Holes
by Ellen B. Jackson (Houghton Mifflin Books, 2008)

Planets, Stars, and Galaxies: A Visual Encyclopedia of Our Universe
by David A. Aguilar (National Geographic Society, 2007)

INDEX

ACKNOWLEDGMENTS

The publishers acknowledge the following sources for illustrations. Credits read from top to bottom, left to right, on their respective pages. All illustrations, maps, charts, and diagrams were prepared by the staff unless otherwise noted.

Cover: NASA, ESA, and J. Maíz Apellániz, Instituto de Astrofísica de Andalucía, Spain

1   NASA/Swift/Aurore Simonnet

4-5   NASA/CXC/CfA/R. Tuellmann et al./AURA/STScI

6-7   © Andrew Zachary Colvin

8-9   © Claus Lunau, FOCI/Bonnier/Photo Researchers; © Don Dixon

10-11 © Noel Powell, Shutterstock; WORLD BOOK illustration by Steven Karp; NASA

12-13 © Shutterstock

14-15 NASA/GSFC; WORLD BOOK illustration; NASA/JPL-Caltech/J. Rho (SSC/Caltech)

16-17 WORLD BOOK illustration; NASA/ESA/Hans Van Winckel, Catholic University of Leuven, Belgium/Martin Cohen, University of California, Berkeley; WORLD BOOK illustration by Matt Carrington

18-19 NASA/CXC/PSU/S. Park & D. Burrows/STScI/CfA/P. Challis; NASA/Aurore Simonnet, Sonoma State University

20-21 ESO; NASA; NASA, ESA, H. Hammel (SSI, Boulder, CO) and the Jupiter Impact Team; NASA/ESA/L. Bradley (JHU)/R. Bouwens (UCSC)/H. Ford (JHU)/G. Illingworth (UCSC); NASA/JPL-Caltech/R. Gutermuth, Harvard-Smithsonian Center for Astrophysics; NASA/CXC/Univ. of Maryland/A. S. Wilson et al./Pal. Obs. DSS; IR: NASA/JPL-Caltech; VLA: NRAO/AUI/NSF; X-ray: NASA/CXC/Wesleyan Univ./R. Kilgard et al.; UV: NASA/JPL-Caltech; Optical: NASA/ESA/S. Beckwith & Hubble Heritage Team (STScI/AURA); IR: NASA/JPL-Caltech/ Univ. of AZ/R. Kennicutt

22-23 NASA/WMAP Science Team

24-25 WORLD BOOK illustration by Matt Carrington

26-27 NASA/WMAP Science Team; ESA; ESA, LFI - HFI Consortia/Axel Mellinger

28-29 NASA/ESA/The Hubble Key Project Team/ The High-Z Supernova Search Team;

NASA/ESA/K. Sharon (Tel Aviv University) and E. Ofek (Caltech); WORLD BOOK illustration

30-31 NASA/CXC/SAO/STScI/JPL-Caltech; WORLD BOOK illustration by Matt Carrington

32-33 © Mark Garlick, SPL/Photo Researchers; © Pierre Auger Observatory; WORLD BOOK illustration by Rolin Graphics

34-35 NASA/D. Berry; NASA/Swift/Aurore Simonnet; NASA/Swift/Stefan Immler; NASA/Swift/Mary Pat Hrybyk-Keith and John Jones

36-37 NASA/ESA/STScI, A. Field; NASA/CXC/SAO/A. Vikhlinin et al.

38-39 WORLD BOOK illustration by Matt Carrington

40-41 NASA/ESA/R. Massey (California Institute of Technology); NASA/ESA/CXC/M. Brada (University of California, Santa Barbara), and S. Allen (Stanford University); NASA/WMAP science team

42-43 NASA/Aurore Simmonet/Sonoma State University; WORLD BOOK illustration by Matt Carrington; NASA/CXC/MIT/Frederick K. Baganoff et al.

44-45 © CERN PhotoLab

46-47 ESO; © David Hardy, Astroart

48-49 NASA/Cassini Imaging Team/SSI/JPL/ESA; NASA; Seth Shostak, SETI Institute

50-51 NASA/Hubble Heritage Team (STScI/AURA), Y. Chu (UIUC) et al.; WORLD BOOK illustration by Matt Carrington

52-53 NASA/WORLD BOOK illustration by Luke Haddock

54-55 WORLD BOOK illustration by Luke Haddock; WORLD BOOK illustration by Matt Carrington; WORLD BOOK illustration by Brenda Tropinski

56-57 © AFP/Getty Images; WORLD BOOK illustration; © Shutterstock

58-59 WORLD BOOK illustration by Matt Carrington; NASA, Les Bossinas (Cortez III Service Corp.), 1998; Courtesy of Andrew Cox